Darn it!

Darn it!

Traditional female skills that every man should know

SARAH WILLIAMS

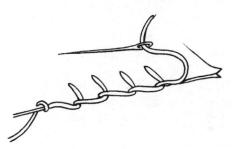

Michael O'Mara Books Limited

First published in Great Britain in 2013 by
Michael O'Mara Books Limited
9 Lion Yard
Tremadoc Road
London SW4 7NQ

A CIP catalogue record for this book is available from the British Library.

Papers used by Michael O'Mara Books Limited are natural, re-cyclable products made from wood grown in sustainable forests. The manufacturing processes conform to the environmental regulations of the country of origin.

978-1-78243-117-6 in hardback print format
978-1-78243-120-6 in ePub format
978-1-78243-121-3 in Mobipocket format

1 3 5 7 9 10 8 6 4 2

Jacket design by Greg Stevenson
Illustrations by Aubrey Smith
Designed and typeset by Design 23

Printed and bound by CPI Group (UK) Ltd, Croydon, CR0 4YY

www.mombooks.com

Contents

Contents

Conversion Tables

KNITTING NEEDLES		WEIGHT	
UK (mm)	**US**	**Metric**	**Imperial**
2.0	0	15 g	^{1}2 oz
2.25	1	25 g	1 oz
2.75	2	40 g	1^{1}2 oz
3.0	-	50 g	2 oz
3.25	3	85 g	3 oz
3.5	4	115 g	4 oz
3.75	5	145 g	5 oz
4.0	6	175 g	6 oz
4.5	7	200 g	7 oz
5.0	8	225 g	8 oz
5.5	9	250 g	9 oz
6.0	10	285 g	10 z
6.5	10^{1}2	350 g	12 oz
7.0	-	375 g	13 oz
7.5	-	400 g	14 oz
8.0	11	425 g	15 oz
9.0	13	450 g	1 lb
10.0	15	550 g	1^{1}4 lb
12.0	17	675 g	1^{1}2 lb
16.0	19	750 g	1^{3}4 lb
19.0	35	900 g	2 lb
25.0	50	1.3 kg	3 lb
		1.8 kg	4 lb
		2.25 kg	5 lb

MEASUREMENTS

Metric	Imperial
5 mm	$\frac{1}{4}$ in
1 cm	$\frac{1}{2}$ in
2.5 cm	1 in
5 cm	2 in
7.5 cm	3 in
10 cm	4 in
12.5 cm	5 in
15 cm	6 in
18 cm	7 in
20 cm	8 in
23 cm	9 in
25 cm	10 in
30 cm	12 in

OVEN TEMPERATURES

Celsius	Fan Assisted	Fahrenheit	Gas
110°C	Fan 90°C	225°F	Gas $\frac{1}{4}$
120°C	Fan 100°C	250°F	Gas $\frac{1}{2}$
140°C	Fan 120°C	275°F	Gas 1
150°C	Fan 130°C	300°F	Gas 2
160°C	Fan 140°C	325°F	Gas 3
180°C	Fan 160°C	350°F	Gas 4
190°C	Fan 170°C	375°F	Gas 5
200°C	Fan 180°C	400°F	Gas 6
220°C	Fan 200°C	425°F	Gas 7
230°C	Fan 210°C	450°F	Gas 8
240°C	Fan 220°C	475°F	Gas 9

LIQUIDS

Metric	Imperial
15 ml	$\frac{1}{2}$ fl oz
25 ml	1 fl oz
50 ml	2 fl oz
75 ml	3 fl oz
100 ml	$3\frac{1}{2}$ fl oz
125 ml	4 fl oz
150 ml	5 fl oz ($\frac{1}{4}$ pint)
175 ml	6 fl oz
200 ml	7 fl oz
225 ml	8 fl oz
250 ml	9 fl oz
300 ml	10 fl oz/$\frac{1}{2}$ pint
350 ml	12 fl oz
400 ml	14 fl oz
450 ml	16 fl oz/$\frac{3}{4}$ pint
500 ml	18 fl oz
568 ml	20 fl oz/1 pint
600 ml	1 pint milk
700 ml	$1\frac{1}{4}$ pints
850 ml	$1\frac{1}{2}$ pints
1 litre	$1\frac{3}{4}$ pints
1.2 litres	2 pints
1.3 litres	$2\frac{1}{4}$ pints
1.4 litres	$2\frac{1}{2}$ pints
1.5 litres	$2\frac{3}{4}$ pints
1.7 litres	3 pints
1.8 litres	$3\frac{1}{4}$ pints
2 litres	$3\frac{1}{2}$ pints
2.5 litres	$4\frac{1}{2}$ pints
2.8 litres	5 pints
3 litres	$5\frac{1}{4}$ pints

US CUPS

¼ cup	60 ml
1/3 cup	70 ml
½ cup	125 ml
2/3 cup	150 ml
3/4 cup	175 ml
1 cup	250 ml
1½ cups	375 ml
2 cups	500 ml
3 cups	750 ml
4 cups	1 litre
6 cups	1.5 litres

SPOONS

Metric	Imperial
1.25 ml	¼ teaspoon
2.5 ml	½ teaspoon
5 ml	1 teaspoon
10 ml	2 teaspoons
15 ml	3 teaspoons/1 tablespoon
30 ml	2 tablespoons
45 ml	3 tablespoons
60 ml	4 tablespoons
75 ml	5 tablespoons
90 ml	6 tablespoons

INTRODUCTION

I t is a truth universally acknowledged that most men, when faced with a navigational problem, will do almost anything to avoid asking for help; there's a social danger, it seems, in confessing to a gap in one's knowledge. This recently proved true for a good friend of mine who took it upon himself to replace the buttons on his threadbare coat. Thinking the female sex inherently possess a knack for all things home-made, my eager friend approached another female acquaintance in the hope she might impart a few sisterly tips (i.e. how on earth you sew on a button). But the fairer sex, it seems, isn't quite ready to welcome her hairier counterpart into its ranks for, dear reader, the poor man was mocked. And so it's been left to me to compile this handy instruction manual for the modern man so he may never be laughed at so cruelly again.

Many sources were consulted in the making of this book, not all of them female. In truth, no woman I know can knock up a period costume with the competence and flair of my battle re-enactment friends – all but one of whom is male. Still, there's no avoiding the fact that some skills are considered to be primarily female, mainly because they have long been the occupation of women.

Coventry Patmore's Victorian poem 'The Angel in the House' came to symbolize the feminine ideal: women were very much considered safest when tucked away indoors, devoted to their husband and children.

While for a fortunate few this meant floating about their own homes, busying themselves with tasks such as embroidery or flower arranging, for those less fortunate, this feminine ideal meant working as a long-suffering maid, cleaning, cooking and laundering to keep someone else's house running. However, as dreary and objectionable as this might seem today, the household expertise such women accrued was very fortunately passed on to their descendants, equipping subsequent generations with invaluable skills.

Thankfully, societal norms have been on the move since then and modern man is just as likely to produce a towering soufflé for his dinner guests as modern woman is to change a tyre on her car. But the gaping chasm between the sexes is yet to be fully filled. So, if you've ever sat feeling helpless after dropping a glass of red wine over your new neighbour's fluffy white carpet, or if you're forever being scolded for failing to clean the bathroom sufficiently, this book is for you. Of course, if you'd rather revel in your ignorance, give it to the woman in your life – she probably doesn't know how to darn a pair of socks either.

CRAFT AND MAKE-DO

The Arts and Crafts Movement began in England around 1860 in reaction to the advent of the Industrial Revolution and the fear that mass production was endangering the skill and creativity involved in making bespoke, handcrafted items.

The movement sought to dismantle the divide between designer and maker, encouraging both men and women to take ownership of their creations, which is an ethos I would encourage. When you are making or mending an item it needn't be drudgery; take pride and enjoyment in being the designer and the maker.

Mastering just a few simple techniques opens up a raft of creative opportunities. Whether it's knitting your own winter woollies, crafting a pair of curtains or pulling apart an old garment – some very ugly cardigans can be made from the finest wool – to make something entirely new, you won't regret welcoming craft and make-do into your life.

Knitting

While thoughts of knitting might conjure up images of your granny clacking away on an ancient pair of needles, or that pile of unwanted Christmas jumpers waiting patiently to be taken to the charity shop, in recent years the art has experienced something of a comeback. These days the wealth of yarns and patterns available means you can make yourself some incredibly groovy attire with very little effort. And what better reward than smugly informing someone that the jumper they've just complimented you on was in fact made by yours truly.

If the idea of knitting makes you a little nervous, fear not – there really is nothing to it, and with a little application you could be joining the hundreds of men already taking part in the knitting revival. (Not to mention cashing in on the potential hook-ups with the army of lady crafters bursting to help you learn how to knit.)

To start with, I would recommend using a tired old ball of wool (something man-made is fine) because then it doesn't matter if you make a mistake, which, dear reader, you will. And, when you do, simply keep calm and carry on – you can learn how to fix your knitting at a later date.

Choosing your needles and wool

The size of knitting needle you require depends on the thickness of wool you use. Generally speaking, the thicker the wool, the chunkier the needle. The packaging on each ball of wool specifies the size of needle needed, but when you first start out it's wise to use a medium-weight wool, such as double-knit, and a pair of UK size 3.5–4.5 mm (US 4–7) needles.

Casting on

Before you start knitting you need to cast on a row of stitches. This simple process involves knitting a number of stitches on to one needle, which will then form your first row.

1. The simplest way to cast on is to first make a slipknot. Hold a good length of wool in your right hand (about 20 cm is fine) and place it on the palm of your left hand loosely in the shape of a number '4', making sure you have a good length of tail.

2. Grab a piece of the tail (but not the tail end!) and pull it up through the middle of your '4', while at the same time tugging on the main length of the yarn. You should be left with an adjustable loop.

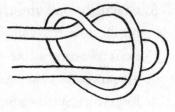

3. Place it on one knitting needle and pull both tails to tighten it.

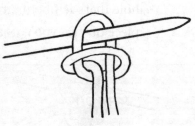

4. Hold the needle with the slipknot in your left hand. With your right hand insert the empty needle from right to left through the loop and underneath the other needle. With your right hand loop the

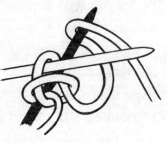

main length of yarn around the top of the right-hand needle anti-clockwise so the yarn is sitting between the two needles.

5. Gradually pull the right needle towards you, but don't take it out all the way – your aim is to catch the loop you've just made. As the loop reaches the end 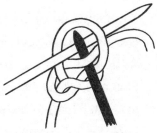 of the right needle, poke the needle back through the hole that's left between the left-hand needle and the piece of yarn you've just wrapped round.

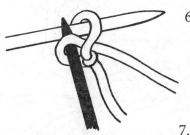

6. The two needles will now be crossing each other with the right needle on top.

7.   Gently tug the right needle to loosen the loop (this just helps you to manoeuvre it) then place the loop on to the left needle.

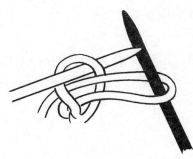

8. You should now have two loops on the left needle and nothing on the right. Well done – you've cast on two stitches! Gently tug the tail of the yarn to tighten the loop and try casting on another stitch, remembering that you'll have to insert the empty right-hand needle into the stitch you've just made (and not the first stitch). Keep going until you have the right number of stitches. Your needle should look something like this:

Knit stitch

Having mastered the art of casting on, you're well on your way to knitting. The only difference between the two is that, when knitting, instead of placing your new loop back on to the left-hand needle as you do when casting on, you keep the new loop on the right-hand needle and take the old one off the left-hand needle instead. Eventually you'll end up with an empty left-hand needle. To knit one row:

1. Follow steps 1–2 above.

2. Gradually pull the right needle towards you and poke the needle back through the hole that's left between the left-hand needle and the piece of yarn you've just wrapped round, as you would if you were casting on. But, instead of transferring the new loop from the right-hand needle on to the left, simply pull the existing loop on the left-hand needle off the end.

3. Repeat this process until you have nothing left on the left-hand needle.

4. To start knitting another row, simply swap the needles around so the empty needle is in your right hand and the needle with the knitting is in your left hand and repeat. This is what's known as blanket or plain stitch. Keep going until you've either had enough or made a mistake, by which point you'll either have created a patch (which you could later hand-stitch to other patches to make a blanket) or, if you're really persistent, a scarf.

Purl stitch

'Knit one, purl one ...' you might have overheard your granny mutter as she crafted another of her knitted creations, but what on earth was she on about? Well, the knit stitch and the purl stitch are the only two stitches you need to knit a garment. Using a different combination of the two stitches – knit one stitch, purl one stitch; knit one row, purl one row – creates a different effect. Take a quick look at the jumper you're wearing. The ribbed pattern at the end of the sleeves is created by alternating one knitted stitch with one purled stitch all the way round. It's good for sleeves because it creates a stretchy knit.

It's a good idea to become aware of how a knit stitch and a purl stitch look. In *Stitch 'n Bitch*, knitter extraordinaire Debbie Stoller likens the base of the knit stitch to a scarf, and the purl stitch to a noose. Here's how they should look:

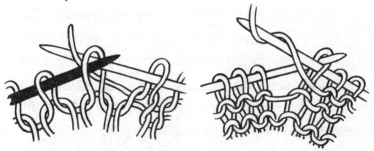

The good news for beginner knitters: purling involves exactly the same technique as knitting. The only differences are:

1. Instead of your right-hand needle going into the loop facing away from you and underneath the left-hand needle, the right-hand needle crosses in front of the left-hand needle.

2. When you knit a stitch, your yarn should be waiting from behind; when you purl a stitch, it should be waiting in front. This is really important to remember and may be the cause of many initial purling-based troubles. Everything else is exactly the same.

Once you can knit *and* purl, the knitting world is your oyster. Here are a few of the stitches you can do:

Stocking/stockinette – knit one row, purl one row. This is the most common stitch and a lovely one too. It creates a smooth knitted surface, and is often used for creating the main body of a jumper.

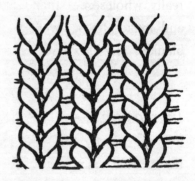

Rib – knit one, purl one. Once you've reached the end of your first row and you're ready to start the next one, make sure you're knitting the knits and purling the purls. Experiment by doing a

double rib (knit two, purl two), a triple rib (knit three, purl three), etc.

Moss – knit one, purl one, but this time, instead of knitting the knits and purling the purls, knit the purls and purl the knits. This is a really wholesome stitch and makes for a lovely blanket.

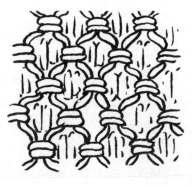

Increasing

If you want to make a piece of knitting bigger, which is usually done at the end of a row, just knit (or purl, depending on the pattern) into the last stitch as usual, but before you drop the knitted stitch off the left-hand needle, knit into it a second time at the back of the stitch instead.

To increase with a knitted stitch:

1. Knit the stitch as normal, but just before you pull the old stitch off the left-hand needle, insert the right-

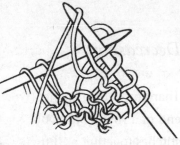

hand needle into the back of the stitch on the left-hand needle.

2. Wrap the yarn around, poke the right-hand needle back through the hole and take the stitch off the left-hand needle. You've successfully added a stitch!

To increase with a purled stitch:

1. Purl into the front of the stitch as you would normally, but don't take the stitch off the left-hand needle. Next, insert the right-hand needle into the back part of the stitch on the left-hand needle with the right-hand needle facing towards you and sitting underneath the left-hand needle.

2. Wrap the yarn around the needle, poke the needle back through the hole and take the stitch off the left-hand needle. You should have created an extra stitch! This is slightly fiddly, but you'll get there in the end, I promise.

Decreasing

Thankfully decreasing (which is usually done at the end of a row) couldn't be simpler. Just knit or purl two stitches together as if they were one stitch, like this:

Casting off

Once you've got to the end of your sleeve, scarf or whatever it is you're knitting, you'll have to cast off your stitches to stop the whole thing from unravelling. It's a simple process, but try to keep an eye on the tension of the wool – too-tight stitches will lead to an asphyxiated cast-off.

1. When you get to your last row, knit (or purl, depending on the pattern) two stitches on to your right-hand needle.

2. Using the tip of your left-hand needle, pick up the first stitch on the right-hand needle and pull it over the

second stitch (think of it as leapfrogging) and drop it off the end of the needle.

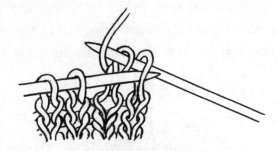

3. Knit another stitch. Pull the second stitch you made (which is now the first stitch on the right-hand needle) over this new stitch and off the end of the needle, as before.

4. Keep going until you have one stitch remaining on the right-hand needle. Cut the yarn (leaving a tail of approximately 10 cm) and pull it through the stitch until secure.

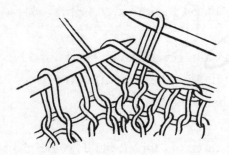

Darning

Having mastered the art of knitting, you're no doubt well on your way to creating yourself a pair of cosy woollen socks, or a splendid pair of gloves to give to your significant other. But it's inevitable that such items, no matter how well made, will at some point acquire a hole. Darning will equip you with the skills you need to deal with such problems so your creations stop short of landfill.

Darning is a versatile skill that can get very fancy, but since our aim is to mend holes and not make lace, I've kept things basic. The idea is to stretch the hole with the darning mushroom and fill in the area by creating a lattice effect with your chosen yarn.

The following instructions are for right-handed folk. If you're left-handed, simply reverse them.

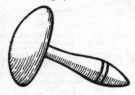

Tools and equipment

A darning mushroom: you can also use a darning egg, which doubles as a very attractive ornament. If you have neither of these to hand, fear not – a light bulb, doorknob, orange or anything else solid and spherical will do.

Thread: In terms of thread, you can use pretty much anything as long as it is fairly hardy and similar in thickness to the material the garment is made from. You can use the original yarn, if the item is home-made and you have any left over, otherwise sock yarn or embroidery thread are fine. You can also buy specialist darning thread, traditionally called 'mending', which some folk highly recommend.

A specialist darning, embroidery or yarn needle: make sure the end is blunt and the needle has a large eye.

Method

1. Turn the sock inside out. Insert the darning mushroom and gather the rest of the sock fairly tightly around the mushroom handle.

2. Starting 2–3 cm from the right-hand side of the hole, insert the needle underneath a loop of yarn, leaving a 6 cm tail of thread. Weave the thread over and under the loops and in a straight line until you reach 2-3 cm beyond the edge of the hole at the other side.

3. Leaving a small loop of yarn at the end of the row (this is necessary in case of shrinkage), repeat the process but in the opposite direction. Make sure 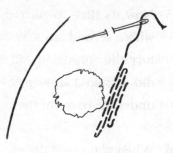 you leave a space approximately the same size as your chosen yarn (roughly one stitch) between your first and second row, and remember to alternate your stitches so the new stitch isn't adjacent to a stitch on the previous row.

4. Continue in this fashion until you cover the entire hole and 2–3 cm to the left-hand side of it. Make sure not to pull tightly on the yarn, especially when you're darning the hole – the patch is replacing the space left behind.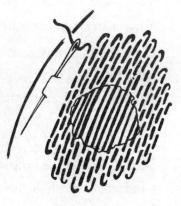

5. Now it's time to go over your first layer of darning with a second layer. With your needle still engaged, turn the mushroom 90° and insert the needle as you did in step 2. Alternately weave the yarn over and under the backs of the loops.

6. When you reach the end of the row, leave a loop, as before, and repeat the process but in the opposite direction. You're creating a lattice, so remember that in this row, and all other alternate rows, pick up the strands of yarn you passed over in the previous row. Remember too that it's vital you catch all the loops during this second stage because an empty loop will create another hole.

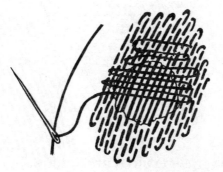

7. Once you've reached the 2–3 cm beyond the other side of the hole, secure your ends (if you're using yarn, just weave them in) and you're good to go.

Duplicate stitch darning

This process is a little trickier than traditional darning, but well worth the effort. It's good for mending socks and jumpers showing early signs of wear and tear, but not for mending big holes. One very important thing to note: the garment you're mending needs to have been made in stockinette stitch (see page 26).

1. With the right side of the garment facing you, insert your darning mushroom and follow instructions 2–4 on pages 33–34. This grid of horizontal lines will provide a framework for the duplicate stitches you're now going to create.

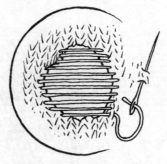

2. When the grid is in place, work your way to the top right-hand corner of the worn fabric, a couple of stitches above the edge.

3. Bring your needle through to the front, directly below the point of one of the 'v' shapes that are made with stockinette stitch. Pass your needle through both arms of the 'v' and pull the yarn through. Now pass the needle back through the point of the 'v' where it first came out. Well done – you've duplicated a stitch.

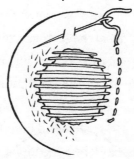

4. Bring the needle through to the front again through the point of the 'v' on the next stitch down and in the same row and repeat step 3. Continue in this manner until you reach the edge of the hole, keeping an eye on the tension of your wool – try to keep your stitches the same size as the originals.

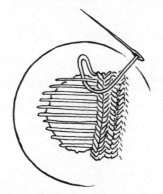

5. Once you reach the worn area or small hole, use the grid as your guide, taking your yarn underneath the first guideline, then back up through the arms of the 'v' above. Repeat until you reach the bottom of the hole. Here you should duplicate a couple of stitches as you did at the top and then weave your yarn in and out of the guidelines to take you back to the top. Remember to arrange your columns neatly as you go and keep an eye on the tension – you want to replicate the density of the stitches in the rest of the garment.

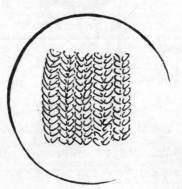

6. Continue until you reach 2–3 rows beyond the worn area. Weave in the ends and you're done. You should be feeling pretty pleased with yourself.

Using a Sewing Machine

Do not be afraid: the sewing machine is an easier beast to master than you might think. Although I'm now a convert, this hasn't always been the case: I was so horrified by sewing machines at school that I managed to charm the teaching assistant into completing all of my textiles projects for me.

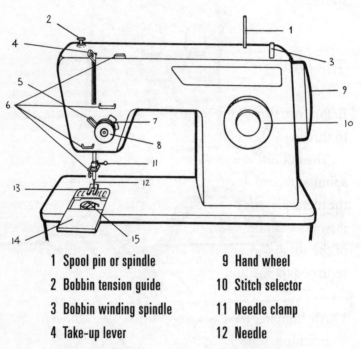

1 Spool pin or spindle	9 Hand wheel
2 Bobbin tension guide	10 Stitch selector
3 Bobbin winding spindle	11 Needle clamp
4 Take-up lever	12 Needle
5 Thread check spring	13 Presser foot
6 Thread guides	14 Slide plate
7 Tension discs	15 Bobbin case
8 Tension regulator	

Let's face it, making or mending items by hand is all very nice but it can take for ever to finish. However, the beauty of a sewing machine is that you can sew things in minutes, leaving you more time to relax and have a beer with your friends.

This diagram of a standard sewing machine shows you all the parts you need to know in order to get started.

The bobbin

Before you thread the top part of the machine you need to thread the bobbin.

The bobbin is a small cylindrical vessel that holds a spool of thread. It sits in the bed of the machine, under the metal plate that resides directly below the needle, and it works with the main thread to provide the underside of the stitch. A bobbin must be loaded with thread and returned to position in order for the machine to work.

1. All bobbins have a case – some are built into the machine, others are removable. Firstly, remove the bobbin, which will involve either opening a door or sliding open the metal plate. There may be a latch you will have to lift in order to access it or it may lift straight out.

2. Select the spool of thread you wish to load on to your bobbin – this is usually the same colour as the top thread – and place it on to the spindle at the top of the machine. Secure the thread with the little plastic holder, if applicable.

3. Take the end of the thread and place it around the bobbin tension spring, the location of which may vary. There might also be one or two thread guides to pass through as well. This again will vary according to the machine, so do check your manual.

4. Poke the end of the thread though the pin hole on the top of the bobbin, then place the bobbin firmly on to its winding spindle – again, located either on the top, side or front of the machine arm. There may also be a bobbin winding position on the stitch selector.

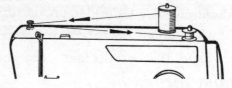

5. Before you start winding the thread on to the bobbin, you normally have to disengage the needle mechanism, which is done by either pushing, pulling or twisting the centre of the hand wheel. Sometimes the bobbin spindle needs to be pushed over to one side in order to work.

6. Keep hold of the thread that's sticking out of the pin hole and put your foot to the pedal to begin winding. You can either stop winding as soon as you think there's enough thread on the bobbin, or wait until the bobbin is full and stops itself automatically. Snip off the thread close to the pin hole on the top of the bobbin and insert the bobbin back into its case. A quick trick for knowing the right way to reinsert the bobbin is to hold it up in front of you with the thread dangling on the left-hand side in the shape of a 'p'.

7. Whether the bobbin case is built in or removable, there will be a small metal latch that has to catch the thread. Leave the loose end of the thread hanging freely. Put the bobbin back securely where it lives, but do not close the door or the metal plate, whichever is applicable. Re-engage the needle via the hand wheel and disengage the bobbin spindle.

Threading the machine

Once you've got the knack of threading a sewing machine you'll be able to do it with your eyes closed. Bear in mind that the method for threading the top part of a machine differs according to the make, so make sure you check the manual for your machine before you begin.

1. With the spool of cotton placed securely on its spindle, take the end of the thread and pass it through the first guide – which should be the next obstacle you come to as you move left along the machine arm.

2. Bring the thread down to the front of the machine and under the tension regulator – a dial with numbers on it, near the needle end – and position it carefully between the two tension discs, which will lie either behind or to the right.

3. On the left of the tension regulator there should be a little hook, and near that an eyelet (which is the thread check spring). Bring the thread out to the front of the little hook and through the check spring (the position of which may vary).

4. Take it back up and through, right to left, the eye of the take-up level at the top left – this lever moves up and down.

5. Bring it down through the thread guides at the nose of the machine and on the needle clamp. Then pull through the eye of the needle, left to right, leaving at least a 3-inch tail.

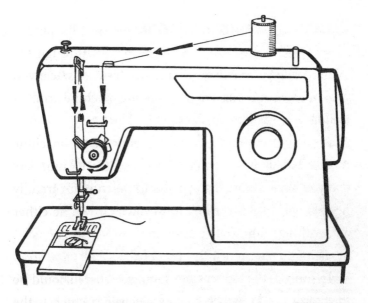

6. Now you have to bring the bobbin thread up. Begin by slowly rotating the hand wheel towards you. The needle will move down, and the top thread will loop around the bobbin and back up, taking – hopefully – the bottom thread with it.

7. When the two threads emerge through the hole in the plate below the pressure foot, shout 'Eureka', grab hold of them and lay them to the back of the machine. When you start to work, keep a gentle hold of them to prevent them from tangling.

Tension, pressure and feed

When sewing, reaching the correct level of tension is very important. But I'm not talking about that tight feeling you get between your shoulders as you realize you've gone wrong – I'm talking about tension in the thread. Too tight and you'll be short of thread, too loose and you'll have more than you bargained for. The tension needed will vary according to the fabric and thread you are working with, so it's a good idea to get into the habit of testing the tension with a bit of fabric before you start.

In short, if the top tension is too tight, the links where the bottom and top threads entwine, which are normally invisible, appear on the surface of the fabric. This may also mean the tension on the bobbin thread is lacking. When the top tension is too loose, or there is too much tension on the bobbin thread, the links will sit at the bottom.

When you adjust the tension, make sure the machine is threaded and the pressure foot is down.

1. Try the top tension first. This is controlled by the tension discs, which are in turn controlled by the tension regulator (a dial or a keypad on modern machines and a screw or a knob on older ones). 4 or 5 is standard, but go higher if your thread is particularly thin, or lower for thicker thread.

2. If this doesn't quite solve things, take a look at the bobbin thread tension, which might take the form of a screw on the tension spring of the bobbin case (for both built-in and removable). It is likely that this will only need a little adjustment, so ensure you make only small quarter-turn adjustments to the bobbin screw – clockwise for higher, anticlockwise for lower. And, again, do so after the case has been threaded.

1 Tension adjusting screw
2 Tension spring

3. The pressure on the foot is regulated either automatically or manually (either by a dial on the side or top, or by a screw or push bar on top of the machine, directly above the needle). Generally, if the fabric you are sewing is lightweight, then the pressure on the foot must be lighter (the lower digits on a dial) and vice versa for heavy fabrics.

4. The feed moves the fabric along for you, but your left hand must always be on deck to escort it. But

be mindful of the speed and consistency with which you do so. The heavier your foot on the pedal, the faster the needle will go up and down. If the needle is moving fast but you aren't helping to guide the fabric through at the same speed, this may cause a pile-up. Make sure you guide the material steadily and with confidence – do not drag the fabric, but don't hold it back either.

Now it's over to you. Grab yourself a scrap of fabric, get that pedal to the floor and start experimenting. Once you're comfortable operating the machine, explore the Internet for tutorials on things to make. You'll have cobbled together your first man bag before you know it.

Hand Sewing Two Pieces of Fabric Together

The eighteenth-century English aristocrat and writer Lady Mary Wortley Montagu wrote about the advantages of women learning to read and write. Lady Mary also considered it 'as scandalous for a woman not to know how to use a needle, as it is for a man not to know how to use a sword'. Well, in these modern times, I think it is as scandalous for a woman not to know how to wield a sword, as it is for a man not to know how to wield a needle. Actually, I don't advocate anyone wielding swords...

Joking aside, mastering basic hand-sewing skills will put you ahead of most other chaps. Within this section you will learn several different hand stitches for joining together two bits of fabric. If your fabric is tough then you will require a sturdy stitch to complement it, such as backstitch, but if it's more flexible your stitch will need to be more forgiving, such as herringbone stitch. One final important point: keep your stitches consistent, especially if they are going to end up on show.

Tools and equipment

a needle
sewing thread
two pieces of scrap fabric

Method

1. Cut off a length of thread (approximately 60 cm is fine, or however much you think you might need) and place it through the eye of the needle. Tie a knot at the bottom of the longer length of thread to hold it in place. Although threading a needle is a simple and fairly straightforward process, it can take a few goes before you get the knack. Wetting the end of the cotton helps, but if you're still having trouble you might want to purchase a needle threader. And keep an eye out for the thickness of your thread – avoid using thick thread on very fine fabric.

2. A basic **running stitch** is very simple to master and is often used to temporarily secure two pieces of fabric together before taking it to a sewing machine. Simply run your needle in and out of the fabric to create a run of similarly sized stitches. You can also use it to create a little pouch: sew a length of running stitches around the circumference of a circular piece of fabric, leaving a tail of thread at the beginning and the end. Simply pull the two tails and you have a pouch.

3. Unlike running stitch, **backstitch** is strictly non-stretchy, so it's a good one to use if you want to create a secure seam. Working from right to left, make a stitch as you would if you were doing running stitch, but when you bring the needle back through to the front, guide it through the point where the last stitch ended. And repeat. On the back of the fabric you should see the overlapping, and on the right side a row of neat little stitches.

4. **Appliqué stitch** is a little stitch that acts like a hinge. It is used for attaching a folded edge to another piece of fabric, which makes it ideal for linings. Again, working from right to left, bring your thread through to the right side, a little below the fold in the top layer of fabric. Guide the needle directly upwards and then back out just above the fold. And repeat.

5. **Blanket stitch** is used at the edge of a piece of fabric, either for decoration or for finishing raw edges. It's an easy stitch to master but convoluted to explain, so

I've broken it down into two manageable chunks:

a. Pull your thread though to the front about 5 mm from the edge of the fabric. Guide your needle directly upwards then back through the point at which you started and anchor the stitch by poking your needle through the loop you've just made.

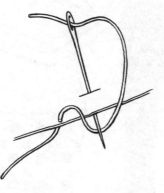

b. Insert the needle from the top of the fabric one stitch length along from the first stitch and 5 mm from the edge of the fabric. Bring your needle up from the back of the fabric but make sure you pass it through the loop of thread. Repeat.

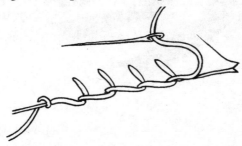

Hemming a Pair of Trousers

We've all done it: bought a pair of ridiculously priced jeans that are a foot too long in the hope you'll one day get round to taking them to the dry cleaners to have them taken up. But hemming your own pair of trousers couldn't be simpler, and you don't even have to own a sewing machine to do it.

Tools and materials

a pair of trousers
an iron
a needle

fabric scissors
pins
thread

Method

1. Put on the trousers and fold under each leg to the desired length. Pin in place then take them off.

2. Cut off the bottom of both legs approximately 2 cm from the new folds in the trousers. Press with an iron. To hide the raw edge, fold the remaining hem allowance in half and secure with pins.

3. Thread your needle with a thread that corresponds with the colour of the trousers. Now you're ready to start sewing with a **herringbone stitch.** Working from left to right, secure your needle in the hem and guide it up past the fold to your right. Make a small stitch in the main fabric from right to left, so that when the thread is taken back down and along it crosses the last diagonal. This stitch is fairly flexible so ideal for hemming a garment with stretchy fabric.

Easy Does It

If this all sounds a bit much, you can buy a fusible web that fixes itself on to the hem with a damp towel and warm iron, requiring no stitching at all.

Sewing on a Button

Surely everyone can sew on a button, right? Well, you'd be surprised how many men have survived for so long without mastering this simple skill. Here's how it's done.

Tools and materials

a garment with a button missing

a button   **a needle**   **thread**

Method

1. If you don't happen to have the original button, find a replacement of the appropriate shape and size.

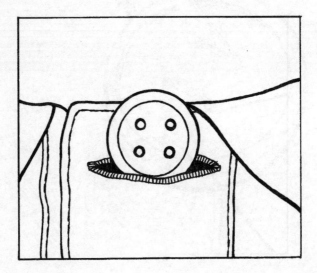

(The back of the sofa can often yield an interesting selection.)If using a replacement button, post it through the buttonhole to check it's the right size.

2. Before you start sewing, line up where your button should go and mark the position with a loose stitch or a dash of chalk. Choose your thread, the colour of which, unless you're looking to make a statement, should match the colour of the button. Thread the needle.

3. Holding the button in place with one hand, use the other hand to bring the needle up through the back of the garment and through one of the holes in the button. Pull until you have just a small tail of thread remaining at the back.

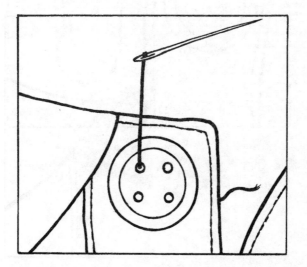

4. From the front, place the needle back through one of the other holes and pull, keeping a grip on the tail at the back. Then go back through the original hole and down again through the second in a circular motion. Tracing your steps like this two or three times should be enough to secure your thread without the need for a knot. Give it a little tug and see – if it's secure, you're good to go.

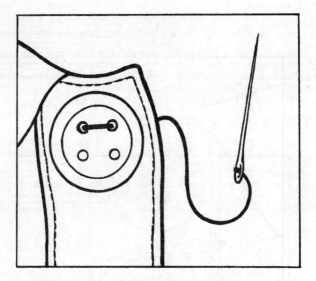

5. If your button has only two holes, repeat step 4 a few more times until it is sufficiently attached (but try not to make it *too* tight). To secure the thread, either tie the two tails together or make a couple of very small stitches in the fabric before cutting the end. If your button has four holes, repeat step 4 a few more times on the first two holes and then move over and repeat this motion on the other two holes so you have two small parallel lines of thread. Finish as for the two-hole button.

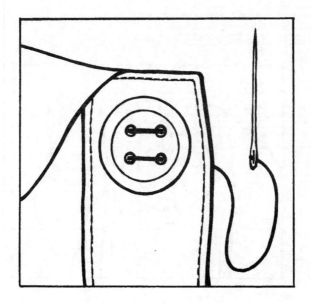

Buttoned Up

For buttons that get a lot of use it's worthwhile making a shank. Simply lay a matchstick on top of the button and sew on the button as normal. Once secure, remove the matchstick, pull the button up and wind the thread a few times around the base before inserting the needle back through to the back and securing as normal.

Wrapping a Present

It's no good buying your significant other (or any other lucky recipient, for that matter) a lovely gift if it isn't presented beautifully. So, here's your chance to wow them not only with your generosity but also with your superior wrapping skills.

wrapping paper   scissors
sticky tape   **a length of ribbon (optional)**

1. Give yourself plenty of space to wrap up the present and make sure you have enough paper to cover it. If you think it might be a difficult shape to wrap, place it inside a box otherwise your finished parcel might not look so attractive.

2. Tear off some strips of sticky tape ready for when you need them – there's nothing worse than trying to hold the paper in place while you grapple with the tape.

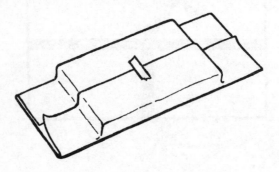

3. Place your present in the centre of the paper and bring one side of the paper over the gift until it is halfway across. Bring up the other side of the paper so it covers the other bit of paper by an inch or two. Stick it in place with a piece of sticky tape.

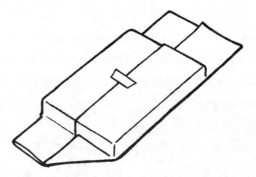

4. Swivel the parcel around so one of the open ends is facing you. Fold one corner into the centre and repeat with the opposite corner. Fold up to close the present and tape securely. Repeat on the other side.

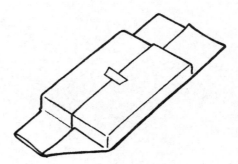

5. If you're feeling fancy, why not chop a length of ribbon (make sure the colour of it complements the wrapping paper) and wrap it around the finished parcel. Simply lay the centre of the ribbon on the top of the parcel across its breadth. Pull both ends of the ribbon underneath the parcel, entwine them and pull both ends across the length of the parcel in opposite directions. Bring round to the top of the parcel, with both ends meeting in the middle. Secure with a bow.

HOUSEKEEPING

They say the way to a man's heart is through his stomach. But what 'they' neglect to tell you is the way to a lady's heart is through a thoroughly well-kept home. So, if you're set to impress, whip out those rubber gloves and get cleaning.

When it comes to housekeeping, I'm very much with Quentin Crisp, who once quipped: 'After the first four years, the dirt doesn't get any worse.' But while the cleanliness of my own nest leaves a lot to be desired, I've certainly done my fair share of housework for others. And it was while cleaning for a man who couldn't abide the smell of powerful shop-bought products that I discovered the wonders of citrus, white vinegar and bicarbonate of soda. Not only are these three ingredients economical and ecological, the combination of the last two products makes a wonderful fizz and hiss, which adds some much-needed light relief to this cleaning lark.

The key to a clean and tidy home is in the upkeep, and a little wipe here and there will save you lots of time in the long run. Prevention, as they say, is better than cure, so if there's a place where water gathers in your shower, for example, make sure you wipe it dry every time you use it or you'll soon have a limescale problem on your hands.

Before you start cleaning, remember to wear rubber gloves, don an outfit you don't mind getting a little mucky and gather together a bunch of rags, toothbrushes and paintbrushes.

Cleaning Kitchen Surfaces

For regular Formica worktops:

Tools and materials

an empty spray bottle   warm water
bicarbonate of soda   washing-up liquid
essential oil   a soft, clean cloth

Method

1. Fill the spray bottle with a mixture of warm water, a tablespoon of bicarbonate of soda, a dribble of washing-up liquid and a few drops of citrus or essential oil. (I recently discovered that lavender oil does not only smell nice, but also boasts antibacterial, antifungal, antiseptic and antiviral properties. Peppermint oil is similarly impressive.) Shake well.

2. Apply to your worktops and floor (if it's lino), wipe with the clean cloth and you'll have a sparkling, sanitized and nice-smelling kitchen in no time.

Wax On, Wax Off

Old socks are perfect for polishing. Slip a sock on to each hand, and use one for waxing and the other for polishing.

An old sock stretched over the bat end of a fly swat is great for getting in tight spaces, too.

For granite, stone or marble surfaces:

Tools and materials

warm water   washing-up liquid

a washing-up cloth   a soft, clean cloth

Method

1. These surfaces require a more gentle approach, and upkeep really is upmost. Make sure you mop up all spillages instantly, avoid placing anything hot directly on to the surface and remember to always use a board for chopping.

2. To clean, dip a washing-up cloth in a bowl of warm soapy water, then dry with a soft, clean cloth. You can also buy specialist products. A very thorough buffing is the key whichever approach you choose, so get that elbow grease flowing.

For wood surfaces:

Tools and materials

warm water   washing-up liquid
a washing-up cloth

Method

1. Wood surfaces require a gentle approach, and again upkeep is very important. Avoid applying direct heat to surfaces and mop up any spillages because liquids that don't evaporate, such as oil, can leave a stain.

2. Clean the surfaces with warm soapy water (or a specialist wood-cleaning product, if you prefer), but limit the amount of water you use if the surface is not sealed. if you want a glamorous kitchen, you must be prepared to put in the labour. Obviously, all wood, granite and other bespoke surfaces can and should be resealed regularly, but that is another book.

Cleaning Kitchen Appliances

For ovens:

Ovens can be a real nightmare to clean, but a little patience pays dividends. Once again, it's a great idea to clean your oven regularly. You can also buy lovely wipe-clean oven liners, which I highly recommend.

Tools and materials

bicarbonate of soda	**water**
a clean cloth	**white vinegar**

Method

1. Mix up a paste of bicarbonate of soda and water and apply it with your hands to the inside oven door and surfaces. Leave to soak overnight then simply wipe off in the morning.

2. If a powdery residue is left behind, wipe with a damp cloth and a little vinegar.

> ### Neat!
> White vinegar, either neat on a cloth or diluted with water in a spray bottle, is an excellent and instant home-made cleaning product. It's also great for bringing out the shine in chrome plated and stainless-steel kitchen products and surfaces.

For gas cooker tops:

Gas cooker tops are easy to clean. Electric cooker tops require a little extra care – watch what you put down on them (piping-hot pans on anything other than the rings, for example, should be avoided), mop up any spillages as they occur and use gentle or specialist products when cleaning.

Tools and materials

bicarbonate of soda	**water**
a clean cloth	**white vinegar**

Method

1. Mix up a paste of bicarbonate of soda and water and apply to the hob. Wipe off.

2. If a powdery residue is left behind, wipe with a damp cloth and a little vinegar.

For fridges, freezers and microwaves:

Tools and materials

an empty spray bottle	**bicarbonate of soda**
water	**a lint-free, clean cloth**
a clean, damp cloth	**white vinegar**
a lemon or fragrant essence	

Method

1. All three appliances can be cleaned inside and out with a mix of 1 teaspoon of bicarbonate of soda to every cup of water and, if you fancy, a squeeze of lemon juice or a few drops of your favourite fragrant essence (such as vanilla essence). Simply wipe on the solution using a lint-free cloth and wipe off with a lint-free cloth.

2. If a powdery residue is left behind, wipe with a damp cloth and a little vinegar.

3. For your microwave, simply place a lemon into a bowl filled an inch or two from the top with water and heat it in the microwave for a few minutes. The steam will make any build-up a lot easier to remove.

Cleaning the Bathroom

Heat and steam are excellent at loosening dirt, so clean your bathroom *after* you've had a bath or shower and you'll be halving your work.

1. Keep a spray bottle of equal parts water and vinegar by the side of the bathtub. Spray liberally on to the surfaces, wipe with a soft cloth and rinse using your shower attachment, if you have one. If you do this often enough you should avoid the need to scrub.

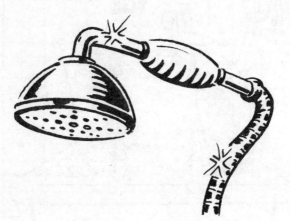

2. For stubborn build-up, leave the solution (perhaps adding a teaspoon or two of bicarbonate of soda, which is excellent at tackling soap scum) to work overnight, or for however long you can afford.

3. The water and vinegar solution can be used to clean

mirrors and windows. Simply spray on and then wipe off with some scrunched-up newspaper or kitchen towel – anything that doesn't leave lint behind. If your windows or mirrors are particularly filthy, give them a wash first with some soapy water or you'll be expending more energy than you need to.

4. Enamel baths are fairly scratch-proof but if you have a plastic or acrylic tub then be careful not to attack it with aggressive cleaning products, scouring pads and/or scrubbing brushes.

5. Cast-iron baths are particularly sensitive and any shop-bought cleaning products containing anti-limescale ingredients can cause the enamel to dull.

6. Vinegar and bicarbonate of soda are excellent at removing odours, so as well as using them to clean with, a little bowl of either, hidden behind your toilet, will absorb any nasties.

7. Tiles and grouting can be cleaned in exactly the same way as baths and sinks. Apply bleach in between the tiles with a paintbrush for extra gleam. If you're going to use bleach, be sure to pay attention to the label.

8. A little dry bicarbonate of soda on a damp cloth works wonders for tap and shower fittings, as does an application of vinegar. The base of such fittings can be a haven for limescale, in which case try soaking a cloth in vinegar or bleach and tying it around the base. Leave overnight.

The Toilet Bowl

Tipping a cup of bicarbonate of soda down your toilet and plugholes on a regular basis will help prevent blockages. Just wash the soda down with a kettle of boiling water and allow it to work its magic. If there's a blockage problem, you'll need to swap the bicarbonate of soda for caustic soda, but this stuff is lethal so do read the packaging. Do not, for example, mix with bleach.

Cleaning the toilet

It's not a job that anybody relishes, but cleaning the toilet is a necessity. And with these instructions you will get it down to a fine art in no time.

a sponge   **cream cleaner**
disinfectant spray   **a clean cloth**
a toilet brush (or something similar)

1. With the toilet surfaces cleared of any ornaments (you don't want them dropping into the bowl) and with your hands safely inside a pair of rubber gloves, you may begin.

2. Dampen a sponge with hot water and run it over the seat, lid, tank and exterior of the toilet bowl.

3. Squirt a cream toilet cleaner around the inside of the bowl and scrub it clean with a toilet brush. Flush the toilet to rinse the bowl.

4. Spray a disinfectant all over the toilet and work it in with the sponge. Rinse off with a clean cloth. Don't forget to give the toilet handle a good scrub too!

Darn it!

Cleaning Walls

For painted walls:

Tools and materials

sugar soap	water
a bucket	a wooden spoon
a sponge or cloth	a clean towel

Method

1. Add approximately one tablespoon of sugar soap to each cupful of water in a bucket and stir with a wooden spoon.

2. Apply the solution to the wall with a sponge or cloth, working from the top of the wall downwards.

3. Once you've removed all of the dirt, go back to the top of the wall and wipe away any residue by spraying with clean water. Dry immediately with a clean towel.

Wallpapered walls have to be approached with more care. You might have received some advice with the packaging but, if not, try the following.

For coated wallpaper:

Tools and materials

warm water	washing-up liquid
a cloth or sponge	a clean towel

Method

1. You should be able to wipe down most coated wallpapers with a solution of warm water and a little washing-up liquid.

2. Be sure to overlap your strokes to avoid streaking. And dry the walls immediately with a towel.

For non-coated wallpaper:

Tools and materials

a piece of stale white bread or an artist's gum eraser
talcum powder   a small brush

Method

1. A piece of stale white bread or an artist's gum eraser rubbed over any stains should remove most dirt without moisture.

2. For the same reason, talcum powder, applied with a brush, will soak up any oily or greasy marks.

Waxworks

If you like to throw the odd party, you should expect to wake up in the morning with, naturally, a hangover from hell and also a few marks on your walls. If there was an incident involving wax, it will no doubt have found its way up a wall, whether the perpetrator was near one or not. Thankfully, such stains can be dealt with fairly easily.

You will need to apply heat to return the wax to a liquid state. A warm (but not too hot) iron is best for this. Simply lay some dry white kitchen towel or brown paper over the offending area and work the iron across it. The wax should transfer to the paper. Try testing on an inconspicuous patch of wallpaper – or, even better, a leftover piece of paper – before you begin. And make sure you wipe both the wall and the brush with a clean, damp cloth afterwards.

If any stains are left behind, apply a mixture of bicarbonate of soda and water to the wall with a clean cloth. If any powdery residue is left behind, wipe the area down with a damp cloth and a little white vinegar.

Cleaning Furniture

The good news is when you come to polish furniture, more often than not a simple going-over with a damp cloth will remove any dust, and a good buff with a clean, lint-free cloth will restore the sheen. In fact, with some finishes, such as polyurethane, furniture polish is best avoided. And try not to use any cleaning and polishing products containing silicon whatever wood you are caring for.

For wooden furniture, it's important to know whether you're dealing with a wax or an oil finish. Wax-finished furniture is significantly less glossy than oil finished. If you're still not sure, wash the furniture with a little warm water and a dribble of washing-up liquid, dry it then scrape the surface lightly with your fingernail – if a little wax comes away then you're dealing with wax furniture.

For wax-finished furniture:

Tools and materials

furniture wax   a lint-free rag
a soft, dry cloth

Method

1. You can buy coloured, clear or pine wax, depending

on what you are polishing. I tend to use a clear wax on dark wood, unless the colour needs replenishing.

2. Apply the wax in the direction of the grain with a clean, lint-free rag (an old sock or super-fine wire wool will suffice). Buff with a soft, dry cloth.

For oil-finished furniture:

Tools and materials

mineral oil	**vinegar or a lemon**
a lint-free cloth	**a soft, dry cloth**
linseed or tung oil	

Method

1. Apply a mixture of a dash of mineral oil and a dash of vinegar or a squeeze of lemon to a lint-free cloth. Wipe across the surface in the direction of the grain. Buff thoroughly with a soft, dry cloth.

2. Apply small amounts of linseed or tung oil to scratches. You will undoubtedly besmirch the surrounding area, so wipe that away before buffing thoroughly.

Cleaning Carpets and Upholstery

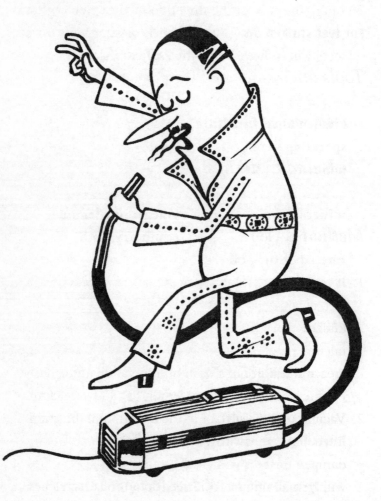

Ideally, stains on carpets or upholstery should be tackled straight away, but spending your time trailing party guests with a roll of kitchen towel is no way to behave.

For wet stains:

Tools and materials

kitchen towel　　**a vacuum cleaner**
sparkling water　　**a clean cloth**
table salt

Method

1. If you're lucky enough to catch the stain while it's still wet, cover it immediately in something absorbent – kitchen towel is good (blot, don't rub), but so too is talcum powder, cornflour or table salt. Cover the area and leave until dry, preferably overnight.

2. Vacuum the area. With any luck, the mess will have lifted, but if it hasn't apply enough sparkling water to dampen the area with a clean cloth. Blot lightly. This will help lift the stain. Once the area is dry, apply table salt to soak up the stain.

Something Different

As an alternative approach to tackling wet stains, add a little laundry detergent or washing-up liquid (the chemicals in shop-bought stain-removal products are damaging to a lot of fabrics) to a bowl of warm water and dab on to the offending area with a cloth. Rinse with a clean, damp cloth then vacuum the area once dry.

My old favourite, white vinegar, is also an effective stain remover. Try swapping this for the detergent if you're dealing with a particularly persistent stain.

For dry stains:

Tools and materials

a vacuum cleaner   **baby wipes or a damp cloth**

Method

1. Before you approach any dry stain, vacuum the area thoroughly to remove any dust and debris.

2. Moisture is the enemy of stain removal and, for this reason, a quick going-over with a baby wipe is commonly recommended for cleaning carpets and upholstery. They work particularly well on leather, as does a damp cloth. Whichever option you choose, always test it on an inconspicuous area first. (And don't forget that sofa and armchair covers might be machine washable.)

For leather upholstery:

Tools and materials

vacuum cleaner saddle soap
a damp sponge a lint-free cloth
linseed oil white vinegar

Method

1. Firstly, clean the area with a vacuum cleaner.

2. Leather can be cleaned rather nicely with saddle soap (often used on equestrian products). Simply apply with a damp sponge or cloth and then buff dry with a lint-free cloth.

3. You can also use a mixture of linseed oil and vinegar to clean *and* polish leather. Simply add two parts linseed oil to one part vinegar and apply with a cloth.

Cleaning Silverware

Even the most basic silver or brass creams, soaks or towels will do a fine job on your silverware and brasses. But I have a couple of other tricks up my sleeve …

For silverware:

Tools and materials

tinfoil	**a tray**
cold water	**bicarbonate of soda**
a soft, clean cloth	

Method

1. Line a tray with tinfoil. Place your silverware in the tray and cover with a mixture of 1 teaspoon of bicarbonate of soda to every half a cup of water. Leave to soak for 10 minutes and then rinse under running water.

2. Buff with a soft, clean cloth and admire your reflection. If your item is too big to clean in this way then simply apply some bicarbonate of soda to a damp cloth, and rub, rinse and dry.

For brass:

Tools and materials

tomato ketchup or lemon and salt
a cloth   a soft, dry cloth

Method

1. Wipe a good glug of tomato ketchup over the brass. (Alternatively, cover a segment of lemon juice in salt and rub over the brass.)

2. Rinse and buff with a soft, clean cloth.

Brassed Off

You can also make a paste of a similar consistency to tomato ketchup of either salt, vinegar and flour OR lemon and cream of tartar to clean your brasses. Simply apply the paste with a cloth, leave to sit for a short while and then ... that's right – rinse and buff.

Washing Clothes

The most important rule regarding laundry is: always separate your whites from your colours. This may seem like common sense, but you'd be amazed how often a red sock (even if you don't even own a pair) can creep into a white wash and turn everything pink. While ladies can pretend they did this on purpose, it's not such an easy look to pull off for the boys ...

Another key point to remember is: group your fabrics as best as possible. A silk garment will require a much gentler wash than a polyester one. So always check your labels, but, at the same time, don't be too precious – a velvet garment, for example, might tell you to always hand-wash, but you'll find it does just fine on a gentle machine wash.

For whites:

It's likely that until you left home, you had no idea that your white garments were so eager to turn grey, and so stubborn about remaining so. Thankfully, the solution is very simple.

Tools and materials

a bucket, bath or sink   water
strong detergent   soda crystals

Method

1. Half-fill the bucket (or receptacle of your choice) with water and add approximately half a cup of detergent and half a cup of soda crystals. Make sure the water doesn't overflow when you add the clothes.

2. Put your whites into the bucket and leave to soak for a good couple of hours.

3. Once your whites are starting to look socially acceptable, wring the bulk of excess water out of your items and wash in the machine on a 60° cycle.

For colours:

Colours can be washed on a lower temperature than whites – about 40° is fine. But if a coloured garment is new, be sure to wash it by hand the first couple of times until you're sure the colours won't run.

105

Tools and materials

hot water
washing detergent
rubber gloves

Method

1. Fill the sink with hot water and a sprinkling of detergent. Add your coloured garments, agitate slightly, being sure to address any particular stains, and leave to soak while you rest and drink a well-earned beer.

2. Return and rinse thoroughly. Alternatively, if you're busy, leave in a sink full of fresh, clean water, and simply wring the item to get all the water out and place on a quick rinse cycle in the washing machine.

Removing stains

Whether you prefer to use soda crystals, bicarbonate of soda, salt, cream of tartar or any of the other household products that work wonders at removing stains, the likelihood is that if it's absorbent, it can help you.

1. Lemon juice and cream of tartar: a simple but powerful stain remover. Make a paste of similar consistency to tomato ketchup, blot it on the stain, leave for a few minutes, then rinse and wash as normal.

2. Shampoo: commonly recommended for collars and anything else blighted by body oils. Rub on prior to the wash.

3. Cornflour: also works well on grease. Cover the greasy area liberally and work in with your fingers.

4. Plain white toothpaste: said to work on grass stains. Apply prior to the wash with your fingers or an old toothbrush.

5. White bread: good for removing lipstick stains. Simply rub on to the offending area.

6. Salt: loosens blood. Either pour liberally on to a fresh stain, or enliven an old stain with fizzy water first (see page 95 for further instructions).

7. Cream of tartar: works well on red wine stains. If you end up pouring red wine on yourself at home (an occupational hazard for some), rather than reach for the white, make a pouch around the area, pour in some cream of tartar, secure and soak.

8. A mixture of sugar and water: a paste made from lots of sugar and just enough water to make it spreadable works wonders applied to a tea stain. Simply apply and leave for as long as you can before washing as normal.

Deodorizer

Bicarbonate of soda is a versatile deodorizer – pour a cupful into your laundry basket from time to time.

Drying Clothes

If you get this bit right, you might not have to read the next section at all. In fact, when drying your garments, I recommend doing everything in your power to avoid ironing them. When items have been machine-washed, this largely involves hanging them with care. Use nice, well-suited hangers (padded where good tailoring is present), do the buttons up and straighten things out where you can.

Here are a few more specific points to bear in mind:

1. Silk items, invariably washed by hand, are best hung up while still soaking. This will eliminate most of the creases.

2. For large hand-knitted garments, wring them out very gently, then lay on top of a towel, pulling and pinching the fabric into the shape you want it to remain (after the first wash you should pin it in place). Place another towel on top and leave to dry.

3. Be wary of drying vivid colours in direct sunlight as the colour might fade. For the same reason, an outside line is ideal for whites. In fact, if you are having trouble returning a white item to its best, soak it in a solution of water and lemon juice before hanging it up.

Ironing

We've all done it – left the house in an unironed shirt in the hope you can pull off that sexy just-rolled-out-of-bed look. Sorry to say though, guys – this sort of attire doesn't wash with the average lady, so it's high time you mastered the art of ironing.

My two basic rules for ironing are: always put on the radio or television before you begin and make sure you tackle the trickiest items first.

1. Use the nose of the board to help you reach those hard-to-access areas.

2. Limit what you iron. My mother irons *everything*: handkerchiefs, socks ... you name it. While I have an unending appreciation for such elegance, I personally believe life is just a little too short.

3. If you choose to iron sheets, fold them first – it reduces the horror.

4. Take your time, especially where pleats, legs and collars are concerned.

5. Develop a routine and take one section at a time. Most people tackle shirts in order – usually sleeves first, followed by the front, the back and then the collar (see below for further instructions).

6. Ironing is best viewed as a strategic challenge. When you win, reward yourself with a treat.

To Steam or Not to Steam?

That is the question. Regarding anything non-delicate, go right ahead. And, if you like creases in your shirts and trousers, then a good steam iron is practically essential. However, for anything too delicate to machine-wash, steam is best avoided as it soaks the item. Again, always read your manual and pay attention to the settings on your iron. If you're unsure about applying heat to a certain fabric, then either turn the garment inside out or, better yet, place another, sturdier fabric on top of it and then iron.

Ironing a shirt

Before you attempt to iron a shirt, make sure it's freshly laundered. Whenever taking clean shirts out of the washing machine or tumble dryer, put them straight on to a hanger and fasten the top button.

1. Look at the label on the inside of the shirt to check what temperature it should be ironed at. Turn on the iron and set it to the appropriate temperature.

2. Remove the shirt from the hanger and undo the top button. Lay the collar out flat on the ironing board and press with the iron.

3. Direct the end of the ironing board through one the sleeves. Press the shoulders. Repeat on the other arm.

4. Press the cuffs then lay one arm flat on to the surface of the ironing board. Use the bottom seam as guidance. Press and repeat on the other arm.

5. To press the main body of the shirt, starting from the buttonhole panel, place the shirt flat on to the top of the board and press with the iron from the

bottom upwards. Keep any eye out for any creases or puckers.

6. Keep shifting the shirt around and pressing from the bottom upwards until you reach the button panel on the other side.

7. Hang it up until you're ready to wear it.

IN THE KITCHEN

History would have it that a woman's place is in the kitchen, but, strangely, those considered great chefs have nearly always been men. Even today, female celebrity chefs are outnumbered by the boys. However, while I have learnt many a top cooking tip from my male friends, I still have a few male pals who live on a diet of sandwiches and takeaways. So for all of you boys out there who think nothing of opening a can of tuna to have for dinner and eating the whole thing straight of the tin with a fork (reader, believe me, I have seen this done), this section is for you.

Food is the stuff of life and making meals for yourself or loved ones can be extremely therapeutic. However, before we go any further, although they say a bad workman blames his tools, there are no free-range eggs in the world that can save an omelette once that pan you've been meaning to replace for years gets a hold on it. And the wrong spatula can not only break a perfectly cooked piece of fish in two, but also your heart – so inspect your tools before turning the page.

Five Ways With Eggs

Eggs are a versatile and tasty food, which you can enjoy for breakfast, lunch and dinner or as a snack. Best of all, they are quick and simple to cook and brim with vitamins and minerals.

My favourite way to enjoy eggs is to slice up a hard-boiled one, mix it with a dollop of mayo, season with salt and pepper and slather on an oatcake – delicious.

Boiled

While boiling an egg might seem the easiest of tasks, a few minutes can make all the difference.

There are, of course, many ways to go about it but the method I describe here is a proven success.

1. Place your eggs in a small saucepan, cover with cold water and bring to a gentle boil.

2. For a soft egg, continue to boil gently for a further minute; for a medium egg, cook for 2 minutes; for a hard-boiled egg, cook for 4 minutes.

3. When you remove your eggs from the pan, pop them straight into a bowl of iced water to stop the cooking process.

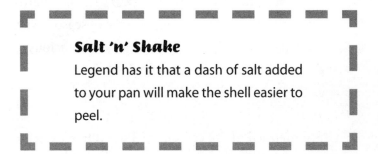

Salt 'n' Shake

Legend has it that a dash of salt added to your pan will make the shell easier to peel.

Poached

A perfectly poached egg can bring the strongest of men to his knees. The combination of just-cooked white, runny yolk and a sprinkling of salt and pepper is heaven on a plate.

And you'll be pleased to hear that poaching an egg is much simpler than you think. The two key ingredients to a perfect poached egg are a decent saucepan or frying pan and some vinegar.

1. Fill a saucepan with approximately 2 inches of water and bring to the boil. Reduce to an energetic simmer

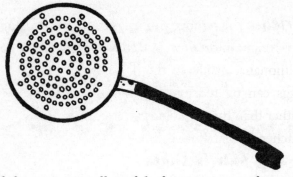

and throw in a small capful of vinegar – one for each egg.

2. Crack the shell of the egg on the lip of the saucepan (be careful not to knock it over) and place the egg in the pan. Try to get as close to the water as you can, but mind out for steam.

3. Keep your eye on the egg. It should take 2–4 minutes, depending on how well you like it done. Don't be afraid to lift it out occasionally with a slotted spoon to check on its progress.

4. Poached eggs taste delicious served on a slice of toast with a handful of watercress. The less healthy but nonetheless out-of-this-world option is to serve your poached egg on a toasted English muffin with a serving of either salmon, ham or spinach and a generous helping of hollandaise sauce.

Fried

Although considered the bad boys of breakfast, fried eggs can be redeemed somewhat by using olive oil rather than the vegetable variety, and drying with some kitchen towel before eating.

1. For the white to achieve that lovely greasy-spoon lace edge, you want your oil hot and fairly plentiful – preferably having cooked sausages or bacon in it first.

2. Once the oil is hot, crack open your egg and place it in the frying pan. Leave for a minute or so, then tilt the pan, pick up some oil on the spoon and pour it over the yolk. Repeat until the egg is cooked.

3. Serve with bacon, sausages and whatever else you fancy.

Scrambled

Although scrambled eggs taste pretty amazing on their own, one of the nicest things about them is you can jazz them up very simply and in a variety of ways. Try frying a handful of cherry tomatoes and chopped spring onions before you add your eggs. Some bacon or pancetta never goes amiss; neither does a sprinkling of chives or a dollop of grated cheese.

1. For basic scrambled eggs, crack open as many eggs as you need (approximately two per person) into a bowl and whisk briskly using a fork. Add a dash of seasoning, a small knob of butter and a splash of milk.

2. Add a dash of oil to a non-stick pan and pour in the eggs. The trick with scrambled eggs is: don't take your eyes off them. Using a wooden spoon, stir the eggs constantly until they are just about done, which shouldn't take long.

3. Turn off the heat and leave while you quickly butter your toast or whatever it is you've chosen to have with them.

Omelettes

There is little else more satisfying than the perfect omelette. And the beauty of an omelette is you can use all manner of fillings to make it tasty. My favourite fillings are either caramelized onions, mushrooms or cheese.

1. Crack your eggs (approximately three to four per person) open into a bowl. Beat lightly with a fork and season.

2. Meanwhile, on a low heat, warm a non-stick frying pan, approximately 10 inches in diameter. Turn the heat up full, add a knob of butter and wait for it to melt.

3. Pour in the eggs and place your filling, if any, into the middle. Bear in mind that the amount of filling you use should be secondary to the eggs. A serving spoonful should be ample.

4. Tilt the pan so that the egg mixture runs to the sides. Agitate the eggs and allow any uncooked egg access to the bottom of the pan.

5. When you see the egg has started to almost set on top (or completely, if you're squeamish), wiggle a palette knife or other appropriate tool underneath the omelette and flip half of it over so it resembles a pasty. By this stage the omelette will be golden on the outside.

6. British celebrity chef Keith Floyd liked to throw another bit of butter into the pan at this stage, but he did die of a heart attack, so the choice is yours.

7. Finally, tip your omelette on to a plate and enjoy.

A Word of Warning

If you're using mushrooms, onions or pancetta, make sure you cook them to your requirements prior to adding to your omelette.

Darn it!

Three Ways With Fish

128

There really is nothing like eating fresh fish, and it's even better if you've hooked one yourself. As well as nourishing the brain, hair and skin, fish is a versatile food, suitable for breakfast, lunch or dinner and, because some very nice fish comes in tins, it's extremely portable. Whenever I go camping, I stock up on tinned mackerel – the breakfast of champions.

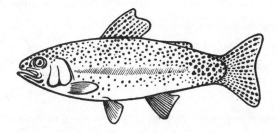

Baked or barbecued fish   *Serves 1*

The following instructions are quite general, so feel free to improvise with flavours and ingredients. You can use any type of fish, whole or filleted, but cooking times will vary, so make sure you check the packet instructions and keep an eye on the fish while it's cooking – when it's done the flesh should flake away when prodded lightly with a fork.

fish
a knob of butter
olive oil
lemon, sliced

a handful of herbs (such as parsley)
a handful of cherry tomatoes
1 courgette, chopped

1. Preheat the oven to 180°C/350°F/gas 4.

2. Wrap the fish loosely in a tinfoil parcel with a knob of butter or a dash of olive oil. Season with salt and pepper and add a few slices of lemon, a sprinkling of herbs (parsley is always delicious with fish) and the cherry tomatoes and chopped courgettes.

3. Place in the oven and leave to cook for approximately 20–25 minutes and serve.

Cooking fish needn't be consigned to indoors. If you're lucky enough to be cooking alfresco, wrap your fish in damp newspaper lined with baking paper instead of tinfoil. Trout tastes delicious cooked with a handful of flaked almonds and a few slices of orange, and cod is wonderful wrapped in bacon.

Kedgeree Serves 2–4

Andy Warhol famously ate a tin of Campbell's tomato soup every day (or, at least, he claimed to), but if you'd prefer to indulge daily in something a little tastier, I couldn't think of a better dish than kedgeree.

1 large or 2 medium-sized fillets of smoked haddock
30 g butter
2 handfuls prawns
2 handfuls frozen peas
2 eggs
150 g rice
1 heaped dessertspoon curry powder (or to taste)
1 tbsp chopped parsley (or to taste)

1. Preheat the oven to 180°C/350°F/gas 4.

2. Hard-boil the eggs according to the instructions on page 120. Once cooked, peel and slice into quarters.

3. Wrap the fish loosely in a parcel of tinfoil with the butter and season with salt and pepper. Place in the oven and cook for approximately 20–25 minutes, or until the fish is done. When it's ready, flake it into a large saucepan along with its juice.

4. In the meantime, place the peas in a saucepan of boiling water and continue to boil for 3 or 4 minutes, or until the peas are just tender. Cook the rice in a separate saucepan according to the packet instructions.

5. Strain the peas and the rice and add to the saucepan with the fish, along with the rest of the ingredients. Stir and serve.

Mackerel pâté Serves 2–4

A little mackerel pâté spread on a slice of toast is a splendid way to start the weekend (or, indeed, any day, if you're lucky enough not to be chasing your tail on a weekday morning).

> **1 packet (2–3 whole) smoked mackerel**
> **150 g cream cheese**
> **100 g crème fraiche**
> **3 tsp horseradish (or to taste)**
> **juice of 1 lemon or lime**
> **a handful of fresh herbs (dill, chives, parsley or thyme)**

1. Flake the mackerel into a bowl, removing any stray bones.

2. Simply add the rest of the ingredients, season with salt and pepper and stir thoroughly.

How to Slice an Onion

As silly as it might sound, using the correct method to slice an onion might be one of the best kitchen techniques you can master. As ever, be careful when handling a sharp knife.

1. Slice the onion in half lengthways and remove the peel.

2. With the root end of one half of the onion facing away from you, make fine vertical incisions across the width of the onion. Make sure you don't slice into the edges of the onion.

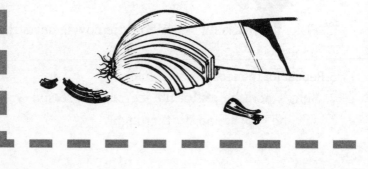

3. Turn the onion-half 90° and make a horizontal slice through the middle, stopping before you reach the root.

4. Slice vertically through onion. As each slice falls away you'll notice that you've chopped your onion into dozens of tiny little cubes.

5. Repeat for the second half of the onion.

135

Two Ways With Vegetables

The following two dishes are quick to create, perfect for both vegetarians and meat eaters, and taste delicious either on their own or as part of a bigger meal.

Stuffed aubergine Serves 2

The king of all vegetables, the aubergine makes a delicious addition to any meat or vegetable dish. Aubergines are also rich in fibre and minerals, as well as bursting with antioxidants and essential vitamins.

1 aubergine
2 tbsp olive oil
onion, finely chopped
2 cloves garlic, chopped or crushed
1 x 400 g tin chopped tomatoes
a splash of red wine
a handful olives, chopped
a generous pinch of paprika
a handful of chopped herbs, such as thyme
or oregano
a teaspoon of sugar, optional
75 g cheddar or 250 g mozzarella
½ cup breadcrumbs

1. Preheat the oven to 180°C/350°F/gas 4.

2. Slice the aubergine in half lengthways. Scoop out the insides using a sharp knife and/or spoon, leaving a 1 cm rim around the edge and the bottom to hold your filling. Place the insides to one side.

3. Smother the newly made vessels both inside and out in olive oil, cover with tinfoil and place in the oven for 20 minutes.

4. In the meantime, fry the onion in a dash of olive oil until translucent. Dice the leftover aubergine flesh and add to the onion. Once the aubergine has nearly cooked through, add the garlic, tomatoes, wine, olives, paprika and herbs and season with salt and pepper. Simmer for 5–10 minutes. If you find the sauce is a little on the tart side, add a spoonful of sugar.

5. Remove the aubergine from the oven and spoon some of the tomato mixture into the shell until it is level with the sides. Lay a few slices of cheddar or mozzarella (or both) on top. Sprinkle with breadcrumbs and place back in the oven for approximately 15–20 minutes.

Stuffed

Peppers, mushrooms, tomatoes and round courgettes can all be stuffed with lovely things. Simply scoop out the middle and stuff with your favourite foods as per the recipe above (but peppers, like aubergines, are best if baked empty or parboiled first). Grains such as rice, bulgur wheat and couscous make wonderful fillings, especially if mixed with chopped vegetables and cheese.

Ratatouille Serves 2–4

The following recipe is the finest ratatouille I've ever had the pleasure to eat.

1 pepper, finely chopped
1 courgette, finely chopped
1 squash, finely chopped
1 aubergine, finely chopped
1 small jar passata
2 tbsp olive oil
half an onion, finely chopped
2 cloves of garlic, finely chopped
a handful of thyme leaves

1. Preheat the oven to 180°C/350°F/gas 4.

2. Grease a ceramic (or oven) dish (approximately 30 cm in diameter if round or 20 cm if rectangular) with a little butter and pour in the passata and 1 tablespoon of olive oil. Add the onion and garlic and season with salt and pepper.

3. Starting from the outside, lay a slice of each vegetable in turn on top of the passata, working concentrically towards the middle. Season again, sprinkle with thyme leaves and drizzle with the rest of the oil.

4. Lay a sheet of baking paper on top (to make sure it fits perfectly, draw around the upturned dish before you begin) and put it the oven for 45 minutes. Serve with your favourite bread or pasta and cheese.

One Pot With Meat

As enjoyable as cooking is, sometimes there's nothing better than throwing everything into one pot and shoving it in the oven while you retreat to your shed/armchair/ the pub for some time out. For this very reason the one-pot meal (or 'casserole', as it is commonly known) is an absolute delight, and it tastes amazing to boot.

Serves 2–4

7–10 new potatoes	**6 sausages**
3 pink lady apples, sliced	**olive oil**
2 red onions, sliced	**1 teaspoon fennel seeds**
1 or 2 sprigs rosemary	

1. Preheat the oven to 180°C/350°F/gas 4.

2. Place the potatoes and sausages in a large ovenproof pot; douse in a tablespoon of olive oil. Place in the oven without a lid and leave for approximately 10-15 minutes, or until the sausages have browned.

3. Add the apples, onion, fennel seeds and rosemary to the pot. Cover with another tablespoon of olive oil, season well with salt and pepper, and give the pot a jiggle. Place the lid on the pot and return to the oven for approximately half an hour. Do check on its

progress from time to time, and toss the food while you're there for good measure.

4. Serve with some nice bread spread with a good helping of butter – a fine way to mop up the delicious juices.

Casseroles

The beauty of a casserole is you can concoct all manner of delicious creations using a range of different meats, fish and vegetables.

But whatever you chose to put in your pot, bear in mind that the starch from the potatoes will lend the dish a certain thickness. And if you swap the apples for tomatoes, and the potatoes for beans, for example, you have a very basic cassoulet (there's bacon in this too), a slow-cook casserole that originates from the south of France. Flour also works as a thickener, and if you need more juice, don't be afraid to add a glug of alcohol and/or stock. Pork and chicken love apples, so cider is always good. And for a rich winter dinner, add red wine to your beef, vegetables, tomatoes and stock.

Finally, whatever meat you are using, be sure that it is cooked through.

Spaghetti alla Puttanesca

'Whore's style spaghetti', as this dish translates into Italian, is quick to make but tastes absolutely delicious.

1–2 tablespoons olive oil
2 cloves of garlic, crushed
5 anchovy fillets, chopped
1 x 400 g tinned tomatoes
1 tablespoon capers
1 tablespoon black olives, sliced
200 g (approx.) spaghetti
a handful of fresh parsley, chopped

1. Heat the oil in a saucepan until it's hot. Add the garlic and anchovies and crush into a fine paste. Be careful not to leave them on the heat for too long (you want to avoid burning the garlic) – 30 seconds to 1 minute is fine.

2. Pour in the tomatoes, the capers and the olives and simmer on a low heat for 15–20 minutes or until the sauce has started to thicken.

3. In the meantime, boil the pasta, adding a pinch of salt (for flavouring) and a touch of olive oil (to prevent the pasta from sticking together) to the pan.

4. Drain the pasta, remove the sauce from the heat, combine and serve with a generous sprinkling of parsley.

White Sauce

White sauce is truly essential (without it there would be no macaroni cheese or a great deal of other delicious dishes) yet it couldn't be simpler to make. All you need is butter, plain white flour and milk.

Serves 2–4

25 g butter
25 g plain flour, sifted
1 pt milk

1. Melt the butter in a non-stick saucepan. Add the flour a little at a time and stir until you have a fairly robust paste. Remove from the heat.

2. Pour in the milk, a little at a time, and stir vigorously on a low heat until there are no lumps. Turn the heat down low, season with salt and pepper and add as much milk as you think you'll need. Continue to heat for approximately 5 minutes, stirring occasionally, until the sauce has thickened.

Saucy

If you're making a macaroni cheese, you might want to add a pinch of either mustard powder or nutmeg, or perhaps a little thyme or sage, not to mention 150 g cheese of your choice. In the case of both macaroni cheese and cauliflower cheese, simply pour the white sauce over parboiled pasta or cauliflower, cover with grated cheese (and breadcrumbs, if you desire) and pop in the oven on a medium temperature until the top turns golden.

Soup

One of the wonderful things about soup is it's a great way of using up leftovers. And it's super healthy and simple to make, too. There are endless types of soup to try your hand at, but they all begin with one key ingredient: stock. The following recipe suggests making stock from the animal carcass left over after a roast dinner. However, vegetarians fear not – you can substitute the meat stock for a vegetable stock cube.

1. Place the carcass into a large saucepan and cover with a litre or two of water (depending on the size of the carcass). A handful of herbs, such as a bouquet garni (a bag of mixed herbs), a generous helping of salt and pepper and some roughly chopped onion, carrot and celery will greatly enhance the flavour of your stock.

2. Cover with the lid, bring to the boil and simmer for at least two hours. Skim the surface of the stock as it's cooking and be sure to keep an eye on the water level – you don't want it to boil dry.

3. When your stock is ready, strain it into another pan and leave undisturbed in a cool place until the fat sets on the top. This might take some time, but it's important.

4. Whatever soup you're making, begin by frying some onion until softened. Leave the onions in the pan and add whatever fish, meat or vegetables you've selected and fry for approximately 5 minutes, then add garlic, if using, followed quickly by the stock. Bring to the boil, cover and simmer for as long as you care to, making sure any meat or fish is cooked.

5. Once it's ready, you can either blend the soup or leave it chunky. Whatever your preference, it's always a good idea to serve it with crusty bread smothered in lots of butter.

Soups You, Sir

Stock can be kept for up to 3 to 4 days in the fridge. You can also freeze it too.

Feel free to experiment with ingredients. Pearl barley is an excellent soup ingredient, and a little cream or yoghurt is an attractive and tasty way to garnish most creations.

Finally, as with a great many things, soup always tastes better the next day.

A rather sober end to proceedings, perhaps, but useful nonetheless, this chapter is here to help you help others (and, when you've been struck down by the dreaded man flu, yourself). The most important advice is: never enter a situation that could compromise your own safety. One injured person is better than two. Some dangers may be obvious, such as oncoming traffic, falling objects, a gas or chemical leak. Others, such as an aggressive person, might be a little harder to spot. Needless to say, the information in this section is for guidance only, so please consult your doctor if in any doubt.

On a lighter note, this chapter embraces the medicinal properties of various plants. Far from being hokum, many of the herbs and spices mentioned here have been used as effective cures for centuries. Mint's medicinal powers, for example, were accepted in Western Europe around the mid-eighteenth century, but first appeared in the Icelandic pharmacopoeias much earlier, around 1240. And the healing qualities of lavender were recognized by the ancient Egyptians, Romans and Greeks.

Bandages

Whether faced with a child who's fallen over and given themselves a nasty scrape, or a slightly inebriated friend who's had a rather sticky encounter with a brick wall, you'll be called upon to apply at least one bandage in your adult life.

The good news is they're very easy to apply. First things first, there are three types of bandages: roller, triangular and tubular. Tubular bandages work in a fairly obvious way, so I won't go into any detail about them here. The other two types of bandage are easy to apply – just make sure your patient is comfortable and that you're positioned so you're not making a nuisance of yourself and follow these simple instructions.

Crepe and elasticated roller bandages

These are probably the most useful type of bandage to use for sprains and other soft tissue injuries as they lend real support to injured joints or tissue.

1. Begin below the injury and wrap the bandage around concentrically a few times to secure.

2. Work up the limb in a spiral pattern, making sure each new layer overlaps the previous layer by approximately half the width of the bandage. Secure the end.

3. On final note, if you're working around a joint, make sure it is flexed slightly and apply the bandage in a figure-of-eight pattern around it.

Triangular bandages

If someone has a badly injured arm they will most likely be in need of a triangular bandage. When fashioned into a sling they help lend support to the arm. Should you need to fashion one simply follow these instructions:

1. Gently place the casualty's arm across their chest and take one end of the bandage under the arm.

2. Take the other end of the bandage over the top of the arm and tie the two ends together at the back of the neck. Make sure it's comfortable before sending your patient away.

The Recovery Position

As well as being comfortable, the primary purpose of the recovery position is to keep the airways clear. If you find yourself in a situation where another person is breathing but not conscious, remembering these few simple steps could save their life. Assuming that help is already on its way ...

1. If there is no sign of spinal injury (if the person has taken a blow to the back of the head or neck and there is pain or loss of control in the limbs or bladder) you can begin. If there is sign of spinal injury wait for the emergency services to arrive.

2. Check that there are no obstructions in the airways and that the tongue is where it should be (i.e. flat to the floor of the mouth). If the coast is clear, proceed by removing any neckwear and loosening buttons or other fastenings on clothes that could in any way restrict the wearer's breathing or comfort.

3. Kneeling in front of the casualty, make sure the arm closest to you is at a right angle to their body and the nearest leg is also fairly straight. Now, take the other arm and place it on the person's chest.

4. Take the leg that is furthest from you and gently raise

it so that the knee is bent, with the foot remaining on the floor. You will then use this bent leg to roll the casualty over on to their side.

5. Arrange the hand that you rested on the chest so that it is under and supporting the head, palm-side down. The most 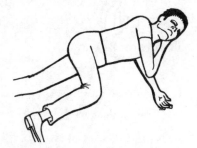 important thing is to tilt the head back and the chin up so that breathing is made as easy as possible.

6. Stay with the person and monitor their breathing and pulse continuously. If no help has arrived within 30 minutes, repeat the process, turning the casualty on to their other side.

Babe in Arms
Injured babies must be cradled, with the head tilted downwards. Airways, pulse and temperature must be monitored constantly.

CPR

Cardiopulmonary resuscitation is vital if someone has gone into cardiac arrest (absent or abnormal breathing to you or me), the function being to keep blood flowing to the brain. If administered correctly CPR can double a person's chance of survival.

1. Call the emergency services.

2. Lay the casualty on their back and make sure their airways are not obstructed or restricted. Lock your hands together, one on top of the other, with the knuckles facing upwards. (If you are attempting to resuscitate an infant under the age of one, use just two fingers.)

3. Place the heel of your lower hand on the breastbone at the centre of the person's chest. Keep your arms straight and start pumping. Press down approximately 5/6 cm (2 inches) and release (but don't lose contact with the body). The British and the American Heart Foundations instruct you to 'press hard and fast to the beat of "Stayin' Alive"'. If you're not familiar with the Bee Gees, this works out at about 100–120 hand presses a minute (or two presses per second).

4. Continue in this manner until the person starts breathing again or an ambulance arrives.

The Common Cold

A bad cold afflicts all of us at least once a year. While of course there's no cure, there are many effective ways of relieving your coughs and sniffles. Pharmacies are lined with products that can treat your symptoms, each containing various assortments of painkiller, caffeine and decongestant. But there are also a host of natural remedies that can be made at home.

A hot toddy

A traditional Scottish drink, hot toddies are usually administered to adults – because they contain alcohol (most commonly whisky, although rum, bourbon and brandy are also used) – suffering from a cold. The combination of alcohol, hot water, sugar, lemon and cloves, is a wonderfully warming combination that helps soothe and numb sore throats.

If you're not fond of whisky, or you like the idea of combining a variety of ingredients, try one of the following concoctions.

1. The main ingredients of a toddy are always the same: hot water and honey. Water purifies and hydrates while the honey helps to sweeten the mixture and it works

wonderfully as a soothing balm for sore throats too. This simple version is great for children, or anyone not fond of spirits.

2. The simplest and most elegant addition is a squeeze of fresh lemon. You could also add cider vinegar – used for centuries as an antiseptic and antibiotic – or some chopped ginger too.

3. In *Jennie's Little Book of Herb and Spice Remedies*, Dr Jennie Charlston-Stokes suggests adding chopped angelica, bruised aniseeds or dried sage to your toddy. The angelica is first added to a miniature bottle of brandy and kept handy in the fridge – it is 1 tablespoon of this that she recommends adding to either cider vinegar or lemon in hot sweetened water. She also says that angelica honey is good for coughs, 1 teaspoon taken every night and day.

4. Dr Jennie also suggests adding thyme and garlic to your toddy concoction, stating it's 'one of the most effective [remedies] available to man'. Simply crush a whole head of garlic and stir it into a jar of warmed honey along with 1 oz (25 g) of dried thyme. Store the jar in a warm place and stir before popping a spoon or two into a cup of hot water.

Drink through it

Toddies are not the only tried and trusted tonics to turn to in the event of illness. Chicken soup is synonymous with colds, which makes perfect sense – sometimes a cold can suppress your appetite, and soup (see In The Kitchen) is extremely nourishing but not a chore to eat.

In fact, anything that's consumed from a mug must be more like a drink and less like a meal, right? For the same reason, smoothies are also really good for you, not only during a cold but all year round. You can pack a lot of fruit and vegetables into a smoothie: celery, kale, banana, ginger and apple is a fine concoction.

Eat yourself healthy

Ultimately, you are what you eat, and if you take pains in your daily life to eat the right, immune-system-boosting sort of things then you're less likely to get struck down in the first place. The two foods that come up again and again in fighting and preventing pain and illness are:

1. Hot pepper (such as chilli pepper, cayenne pepper or jalapeño): contains a multitude of vitamins and has been proven to increase your heat production and

oxygen consumption, as well as being an antioxidant. And you don't have to like hot things to introduce this particular spice into your life. A little sprinkle of cayenne or paprika on potato wedges or in anything tomato-based should do it.

2. Garlic: a friend of mine once administered half a garlic clove to an excruciatingly painful tooth to almost instant relief, and indeed garlic is a miracle cure for a great many things. Antiseptic, antibacterial and a purifier of the blood, garlic does the lot. A recently published study found that a daily garlic supplement reduced the risk of the volunteers catching a cold by half. (NB. Do speak to your doctor before taking this supplement if you are also on blood-thinning medication). One clove a day will boost your body's supply of a range of vitamins and minerals and, fortunately, garlic is essential in many dishes and a welcome addition to most others (see box).

Crushed

Before cooking your garlic, crush and slice the cloves and leave to stand for 10 minutes to allow the allicin (the compound that gives the vegetable its taste and smell) to develop. I always sprinkle with a little salt before slicing too. And always be careful not to overcook it.

Steam

If your nose is blocked and you've forgotten what it's like to be able to breathe freely through two nostrils, inhale some steam to clear out your airways. Although there's special apparatus available for this sort of thing, it's much simpler to fill a basin full of hot water, add a few drops of eucalyptus or peppermint oil and hover your face over the top with a towel draped over the back of your head. Breathe and enjoy.

Rest

Last, but certainly not least, is rest – make sure you get plenty of it. If your body wants to sleep for three days then let it. Only, make sure to take some water with you. (And, if you have a child with a cold, do try to take advantage of any chinks of appetite.) Staying in bed will also ensure that you don't give your lovely germs to friends or colleagues (your family, I'm afraid, are probably doomed already). Having a cold, at its best, is a really good excuse to stay under a duvet and watch black and white films.

Sickness

As a child I remember a friend's mother stuffing her daughter and me with cream crackers after too much fun on a roundabout. I was amazed at the time how effective this was and indeed salted crackers are commonly prescribed for morning or motion sickness.

Motion sickness

Have a nibble on a salted cracker before you depart and keep a box with you throughout the journey. A few drops of essential peppermint oil on the abdomen and/or wrists is also thought to relieve travel-related sickness.

Stomach acid

Bicarbonate of soda is good for neutralizing excess stomach acid. Take a teaspoon dissolved in some water. This is not to be done on too regular a basis (it is high in sodium, after all), however, and if your upset is consistent or you are vomiting excessively then contact the professionals straight away.

Sickly stomach

Mint and camomile tea have long been considered a tonic for sickly tummies, indigestion, flatulence and diarrhoea. They both have an antibacterial effect on the body and camomile is thought to calm inflamed or irritated mucous membranes in the digestive tract. Similarly, cinnamon is added to rich meat dishes in the East to aid digestion, and ginger is a help where all forms of sickness are concerned. Just don't take too much of it because it can cause heartburn.

Stings

Whether it's you or a child that's been stung, it's not a pleasant experience. Fortunately there is a range of home-made remedies to treat all manner of stings.

1. Bee stings: an alkali, bicarbonate of soda neutralizes the acidic content of bee stings. Make a paste by combining with a little water and applying to the affected area. This will also sooth insect bites and poison ivy rashes as well as general skin irritations such as measles and chicken pox. Lavender oil mixed with a carrier oil (olive is ideal) is also credited with relieving bee stings.

2. Poison ivy and ticks: peppermint oil is said to work well on both.

3. Mosquito bites: a mixture of bicarbonate of soda and vinegar will tackle a mosquito bite.

4. Wasp stings: unlike bee stings, wasp stings are alkaline and can be treated with white vinegar, or a poultice of ground basil and water, which also works on hornet bites.

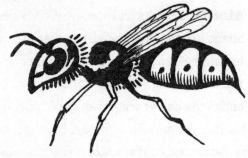

5. For all other types of sting, Dr Jennie recommends tarragon vinegar as a 'super sting settler'. Simply add some fresh or dried tarragon to a bottle of cider vinegar, leave in a warm place for twenty-four hours and then strain into a sterilized bottle. A concentrated solution of camomile, with its anti-inflammatory properties, is also a useful tonic to have about one's person on a summer adventure. Simply brew one or two camomile teabags in a cup full of boiling water and allow to cool. Remove the bags and decant the stewed mixture into a small bottle.

Mouth Stings

Stings to the mouth or tongue can be extremely dangerous. If this happens and the tongue begins to swell, suck on an ice cube/lolly/cream immediately.

Burns, Aches and Other Scrapes

The general rule is if a burn or scald is bigger than your hand then it's a hospital job. Otherwise there are some effective treatments you can administer from your own home.

Sunburn

1. Make a paste with water and bicarbonate of soda and add a few drops of lavender oil.

2. Dilute with sterile water (see box on page 180), decant into a spray bottle and spray liberally on the burnt sun worshipper.

Scalds

1. Place the affected area into or under cold or lukewarm water for 10–30 minutes, depending on the severity.

2. Keep the person warm at all times and cover the injury in clingfilm to keep it clean.

3. Burns tend to sting for a while so administer painkillers as instructed on their packaging.

So Sterile

If you don't have bottled water to hand, simply boil a panful of tap water and allow to cool fully before diluting the paste.

> **In the Event of Severe Bleeding**
> Make a tourniquet out of any material to hand (tearing your own clothing, if necessary) and tie tightly around the wound to stop blood. Then call for help.

Headaches

1. Peppermint oil applied directly to the temples, forehead and/or back of neck can relieve a headache. Lavender is effective too, but be sure to dilute essential oils with water if you have particularly sensitive skin.

2. A warm compress is always welcome for sufferers of aches and pains. Simply dribble a few drops of your favourite essential oil on to a folded wet cloth and place it in the microwave for 20–40 seconds.

Cuts and grazes

1. A good few drops of lavender oil, added to either water or a carrier oil (such as olive oil), is good at soothing most cuts and grazes.

2. Before you apply the oil, make sure the cuts are clean. Apply the oil using a piece of cotton wool then affix a sterile dressing. A plaster in most cases is appropriate.

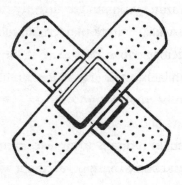

Eye infections

A potion of camomile and sterile water (see page 180 for instructions) is a nice treat for the eyes in the event of infection. Either bathe the eyes or administer a few drops with a pipette. Camomile is also good for toothaches, as is garlic (see page 168).

Be Prepared

While young children will accrue cuts, grazes, bumps and bruises as they learn to walk, slightly older children will no doubt acquire theirs while out to play. While most injuries won't be serious, do be vigilant and keep an eye on any cuts and grazes for signs of infection – usually redness or swelling – within the first couple of days. If in doubt, take your child to see the doctor.

Reading a Temperature

There's only one way to get to the bottom of feeling poorly – whether it's you or somebody else – and that's to get the thermometer out. Whichever method you choose, if a reading is high, wait twenty minutes and then take it again to be sure – body temperature fluctuates throughout the day and is also sensitive to hormone levels.

Oral reading

A normal temperature is considered to be approximately 37°C (98.6°F). For adults, anything above 37.8°C (100.04°F) is considered high. For children, anything above 37.4°C (99.3°F) is considered high. Only children over the age of five should have their temperature read orally.

Armpit reading

For adults, a reading from an armpit will be approximately 0.5°C (32.9°F) lower than an oral reading, and a rectal or ear reading will be slightly higher. An armpit reading is not generally recommended for children as the thermometer needs to be left for five minutes.

Rectal reading

Although not the most fun to administer, rectal readings are the most accurate, especially if checking a child's temperature. Anything above 38.3°C (100.94°F) in adults is considered high. For children, it is anything above 38°C (100.4°F).

Index